Sustained Success
Mindfulness for Achieving Career Goals

Table of Contents

Chapter 1. Introduction

Unleashing your best self isn't a dream, it's achievable with the right mindset! In our exclusive Special Report, "Sustained Success: Mindfulness for Achieving Career Goals," we delve deep into the nexus of mindfulness and career advancement. Your professional achievement has never been more aligned with personal growth and mental clarity. We unveil the calming practices of mindfulness, which can serve as effective tools to boost productivity, enhance creativity, and catalyze breakthroughs in the workplace. This isn't just a report; it's your roadmap to success. Captivating anecdotes and evidence-based strategies make this Special Report a must-read for anyone who's looking to tackle career goals with a renewed sense of purpose and wellbeing. Embrace our Special Report as your resource, and embark on a journey of mindfulness to propel your career towards sustained success!

Chapter 2. Discovering Mindfulness: The Journey Begins

Mindfulness is not merely a buzzword, it's a transformative practice that has the potential to impact every facet of your life—especially your career. The journey to discovering mindfulness begins with a clear understanding of what it is, its origins, the science supporting its merits, and how it can be applied in various fields, notably in workplace scenarios to achieve professional goals.

2.1. What is Mindfulness?

Mindfulness, a concept that originated in the Buddhist tradition, is a form of meditation that involves focusing one's full attention on the present moment. It encourages acceptance of what is, without judgment or overthinking. It's not just about reducing stress or relaxation; it's about getting to know your mind and seeing in a clear, non-judgmental manner. This state of conscious awareness can drive remarkable personal and professional growth.

2.2. The Origins of Mindfulness

The practice of mindfulness has existed for thousands of years, initially tied to spiritual and religious practices, notably Buddhism. Mindfulness as a practice and philosophy was cultivated by the Buddha himself, who promoted 'sati' or mindfulness as one of the core components of his teachings. It was not until the 20th century that mindfulness began to gain recognition as a powerful tool for enhancing wellbeing and productivity in a non-religious context, owing largely to the efforts of individuals like Jon Kabat-Zinn. Zinn's Mindfulness-Based Stress Reduction (MBSR) program, launched at the University of Massachusetts Medical School, pushed mindfulness into the mainstream, proving its efficacy in diverse settings, including workplaces.

2.3. The Science of Mindfulness

Mindfulness has its roots in religious and philosophical traditions, but recent neuroscience and psychology research have provided empirical evidence of its positive effects. Studies have shown that regular practice of mindfulness can result the change in certain areas of the brain related to attention, cognition, emotional regulation, and self-awareness. Notably, it is associated with an increase in cortical thickness in the hippocampus, a brain area responsible for learning and memory, and a decrease in cell volume in the amygdala, the part of the brain responsible for fear, anxiety, and stress. This confluence of increased self-awareness and reduced stress responses can yield powerful dividends in the workplace by enhancing decision-making abilities, fostering creativity, and bolstering resilience.

2.4. Mindfulness in Action: Workplace Scenarios

Fringe benefit or foundation? When it comes to mindfulness, more organizations are realizing it's the latter. An increasing number of companies adopt mindfulness programs, recognizing their potential to improve employee wellbeing and productivity. A few examples of mindfulness in action may help illustrate its potential.

2.4.1. Lowering Stress and Burnout

High-stress environments often lead to employee burnout, which can undermine performance, productivity, and engagement. Mindfulness can combat these effects by enhancing stress management and fostering mental resilience. Employees practicing mindfulness develop their awareness of stress-inducing thoughts and triggers, enabling them to mitigate stress more effectively.

2.4.2. Enhancing Collaboration and Creativity

Modern workplaces increasingly value innovation and fresh ideas. Mindfulness can boost creativity by improving focus, reducing judgmental thinking, and promoting nuanced perspectives. It also enhances empathy and communication, fostering better coworker relationships and more effective teamwork.

2.4.3. Improving Leadership Abilities

Leaders practicing mindfulness often show improved decision-making abilities and empathetic communication. These effects can increase team cohesiveness and productivity, fostering a more positive and productive workplace culture.

The integration of mindfulness into work environments has shown beneficial impacts on individual performance and team dynamics. These are just a few ways that mindfulness can be utilized in the workplace, and research continues to uncover more potentials.

2.5. The Road Ahead: Mindfulness and Career Advancement

As workplaces continue to evolve, soft skills like empathy, resilience, and self-awareness have become highly valued. Mindfulness is a powerful tool for cultivating these skills and enhancing career prospects. As you embark on this journey, remember that mindfulness isn't about achieving a certain state or quick results. Instead, it's about learning, growing, and evolving continually. Embrace mindfulness as an ongoing practice, and you're likely to see impacts that go beyond the office, transforming all areas of life.

The journey to discovering mindfulness has just begun, but the route is already paved with invigorating milestones. In the upcoming chapters of this report, you'll gain more insights into the practices and practical tools of mindfulness for achieving career goals. Bear in mind, mindfulness is not a destination - it's a journey that carries the potential for continual personal and professional growth.

Chapter 3. Mind Over Matter: Connecting Mindfulness and Career Outcomes

In today's fast-paced work culture, everyone is in search of that secret weapon to give them an edge and spur them towards success. That secret weapon is not always a particular skill, currency, or network connection. Many times, it's something far more intrinsic, just waiting within ourselves to be tapped — our mindfulness.

Mindfulness is the ability to be fully present, aware of where we are and what we're doing, not overly reactive or overwhelmed by what's happening around us. When it comes to our careers, leveraging our mindfulness can be a significant tool for advancement and achievement.

3.1. The Essence of Mindfulness

Many people have a skewed perception of mindfulness as being a sort of detachment from reality, where one becomes so 'in the moment' that they lose sight of everything around them. But this couldn't be farther from the truth. Mindfulness is not about separating ourselves from the realities of life but rather becoming more in tune with them.

Let's consider the example of a seasoned mountain climber, making their way up a steep bluff. They are not detached or lost in thought; instead, they are acutely aware of their body, the feel of the rock under their fingertips, the altitude, and their energy levels. They have an intense focus on every moment, knowing full well that one misstep could be catastrophic. This, in essence, is mindfulness: being aware of our environment, our bodies, and our minds, and responding thoughtfully rather than reactively.

3.2. Mindfulness and Career Success

Once we understand what mindfulness is, the next step is learning how to apply it to our career path. Mindfulness, when put into practice professionally, implies using our full consciousness to tackle tasks, make connections, and build strategies.

1. Enhanced decision making: Our day-to-day job involves a series of decisions, both minor and major. Each choice can have lasting impacts on our careers. By practicing mindfulness, we can ensure that we are making the most clear-headed, rational, and beneficial decisions possible.

2. Increased productivity: Research reveals that mindful practices such as meditation can help employees focus better, resulting in increased productivity. Instead of being overwhelmed by multiple tasks, employees can handle one task at a time and get more accomplished.

3. Creativity boost: Studies show that mindfulness practices enable employees to tap into their creative side, leading to more innovative ideas and solutions.

3.3. The Mind-Body Connection and Mindfulness

The mind and body share a powerful connection that plays a crucial role in mindfulness. When we're in good physical shape, it positively impacts our mental wellness, and vice versa. Employees who take frequent breaks for mindfulness activities such as yoga and meditation reported lower levels of stress and higher levels of job satisfaction, strengthening the bond between mindfulness and career growth.

3.4. Mindfulness as Your Secret Advancement Tool

To use mindfulness as a tool for career advancement, start by implementing mindfulness practices in your daily routine. This could be meditation, mindful eating, yoga, or other activities that enable you to engage wholly with the present.

Remember, our brain is a muscle, and similar to other muscles, it needs practice and training to enhance its abilities. Nurturing mindfulness is a progressive journey that develops over time, the outcomes of which can be extraordinary on both personal and professional levels.

3.5. Incorporating Mindfulness in Your Daily Professional Life

Integrating mindfulness into your career doesn't have to mean taking a break every hour to meditate — although taking short mindfulness breaks can be beneficial. It can be as straightforward as dedicating a few minutes at the start of each day to set your intentions or regularly taking deep, mindful breaths during stressful situations to center your thoughts.

Practice being fully present in your conversations, meetings, and tasks. Try to eliminate distractions that prevent you from focusing on the task at hand. This kind of intentional focus can increase productivity and decrease stress.

3.6. Mindfulness Training for Organizational Success

Organizations can benefit from incorporating mindfulness training into their professional development programs. Such initiatives can help employees respond better to stress, be more creative, and communicate effectively. The more an organization promotes mindfulness, the more it can see an uptick in employee resilience and overall organizational productivity.

In conclusion, mindfulness is not just a buzzword. It's a substantive, scientific approach to enhancing your performance, communication, leadership, decision-making skills, and overall career growth. Reframing our understanding of mindfulness from a concept frequently paired with yoga or spa retreats to a viable professional tool may just give us the edge we are looking for in our careers. Mastering mindfulness can truly alter the course of our careers, enabling us to take each step with clarity, purpose, and success.

Chapter 4. Success in the Now: Using Mindfulness to Enhance Productivity

Silicon Valley's titans and top entrepreneurs have often credited their extraordinary success to their mindfulness journey - where the cultivation of a present-focused, nonjudgmental mindset has proven to be an unparalleled advantage. The research supporting the transformative effects of mindfulness on workplace productivity is growing. This chapter provides evidence-based suggestions on how mindfulness practices can enhance productivity, thereby making a significant contribution to career advancement and sustained success.

4.1. The Science Behind Mindfulness and Productivity

Howard C. Stevenson, prolific author and Professor of Psychology and Education, defined productivity as "an employee's ability to produce outcomes, services, or products." Delivering these outcomes requires focus, creativity, and mental resilience—all benefits of a consistent mindfulness practice.

Mindfulness, in essence, is the practice of developing an active, open attention to the present. It is about observing your experiences from moment to moment, without judging or critiquing them. This practice enables you to live in the moment and awakening to experience.

Research shows that mindfulness can reduce stress, improve focus, memory, and emotional intelligence—traits that are essential for productivity. A report published by the American Psychological Association found that mindfulness-based therapy could be beneficial in alleviating anxiety and depression, which impede productivity.

4.2. Integrating Mindfulness Practices into the Workplace

Frequently, the high-speed, high-pressure environment of modern work leads to stress, burnout and reduced productivity. Mindfulness can offer a counterbalance, providing tools to manage these challenges more efficiently. The first step in infusing mindfulness into the workplace is by integrating daily practices that encourage mindful awareness. Some of these practices include:

1. Office Meditation: Encourage employees to take short meditation breaks during the workday. This could be as simple as taking five minutes every hour to sit silently and focus on the breath.

2. Mindful Meetings: Begin meetings with a minute of silence, allowing everyone to center themselves and become fully present before the discussion commences.

3. Mindful Eating: Instead of rushed meals in front of a computer screen, encourage mindful eating—paying attention to the tastes, textures, and smells of food can significantly enhance mindfulness.

4.3. Addressing the Challenges

While mindfulness has several benefits, it's not without its challenges. Integration into the workplace needs to be done authentically and genuinely, not merely as a way to extract more productivity. Mindfulness should be seen as a complete program to enhance overall wellbeing rather than a quick fix to increase productivity rates.

Educating people about mindfulness, promoting its regular practice, and ensuring management support are all critical for successful implementation. Most importantly, it must ensure employee wellbeing is the ultimate goal, rather than increased productivity.

4.4. Seeing Mindfulness in Action

Mindfulness isn't just another corporate buzzword—it's a mindset, a disposition, a new way of operating. It has yielded demonstrable results in major companies worldwide:

1. Google's Search Inside Yourself program, a two-day mindfulness course aimed at improving emotional intelligence, has been completed by thousands of employees and found to enhance overall productivity.

2. Intel's Awake@Intel program showed that employees who participated had a 2-point decrease in perceived stress levels, and a 3-point increase in overall happiness and wellbeing, factors that significantly influence productivity.

4.5. Conclusion

In a world where work-related stress costs U.S. businesses up to $300 billion annually, mindfulness presents an accessible tool for enhancing productivity by promoting a more present, balanced, and focused workforce. This chapter has presented several ways of integrating mindfulness into the workplace and shown how companies are enjoying the benefits. The takeaway is simple—mindfulness is not merely a tool for self-improvement; it's an essential strategy for corporate success. When embraced corporately, it can pave the way to a productive, creative, and diverse workplace where workers are at their best—the key to sustained success.

Chapter 5. Mindfulness and Resilience: Thriving in the Face of Challenges

In an era characterized by stress and high-pressure environments, resilience—our capacity to bounce back from adversity and maintain mental health—has proven to be a crucial skill. Mindfulness, a practice where we purposefully focus our attention on the present moment and accept it without judgement, can bolster this resilience. By integrating mindfulness techniques, we can build resilience to not merely survive the challenges but thrive amidst them, thus paving the path for sustained success.

5.1. The Dynamic Duo: Mindfulness and Resilience

Psychologists have established through copious research that mindfulness acts as a potent resilience amplifier. While resilience gives you the ability to recover from stressful situations, mindfulness ensures that the process is smooth, swift, and less detrimental to your overall mental health.

Practicing mindfulness strengthens physiological resilience by improving stress-related biomarkers, such as reduced cortisol levels and enhanced immune responses. It can improve cognitive resilience by promoting adaptive thinking, as well as emotional resilience through reducing rumination and enhancing emotion regulation skills.

Life's inevitable adversities don't necessarily result in decreased productivity or creativity—provided we have the required resilience to move forward, bolstered by the cornerstone practices of mindfulness.

5.2. How Mindfulness Boosts Resilience

Embracing the present moment, inclusive of all its challenges and discomforts, might seem counterintuitive. However, mindfulness can surprisingly contribute to improved resilience in several ways.

Firstly, mindfulness reduces negative bias, which is our innate tendency to overemphasize the 'bad' experiences while underplaying the 'good' ones. By cultivating non-judgmental awareness of every experience, mindfulness refocuses our attention on the actual scale of the problem, preventing mind-created amplification of adversity.

Secondly, mindfulness encourages the habit of 'decentering'. Decentering refers to the ability to perceive thoughts and emotions as temporary, objective events in the mind rather than identifying with them. This disengagement enables us to respond to adverse events rather than react reflexively.

Thirdly, it helps build self-compassion, which is an understanding attitude towards one's own disappointments and failures, where they are seen as a normal part of life. Individuals who practice self-compassion have been found to show higher resilience levels when dealing with adversity.

5.3. Cultivating Mindfulness for Resilience

Given the profound effects of mindfulness on resilience, it's imperative to understand how to cultivate and nurture these practices. Thankfully, mindfulness is a skill that can be learned and integrated into daily life without needing major life adjustments.

One vital method is practicing Mindfulness-Based Stress Reduction (MBSR), an eight-week evidence-based program that involves meditation, body awareness, and yoga. Another technique is mindfulness-based cognitive therapy (MBCT), aimed at helping people who are susceptible to recurrent depression. MBCT combines mindful practices and cognitive therapy to teach individuals how to break free from destructive thought patterns.

Daily practices, such as mindful eating, mindful communication, mindful walking, etc., are also effective ways of cultivating mindfulness and consequently, resilience.

5.4. Tools for Practicing Mindfulness

To begin your journey towards mindful resilience, several tools can be used. You might consider guided meditations or mindfulness apps. Tools like daily mindfulness prompt cards, mindful coloring books, or calming mindfulness music can be effective for individuals who find traditional sitting meditation challenging. It's essential to remember that the key here is consistency rather than the length of mindfulness sessions.

5.5. Resilience Through Mindfulness: Practical Examples

There are numerous examples across various sectors of individuals using mindfulness to build resilience and thrive in adversity. For example, mindfulness-based resilience training has been beneficial in fields that involve high value-based stress, such as healthcare. Meanwhile, Fortune 500 companies conduct mindfulness training to build resilience, improve decision-making skills, and foster their employees' overall well-being.

Practicing the calming art of mindfulness can dramatically elevate your resilience, enabling you to handle workplace challenges with equanimity and grace. Giving mindfulness a place in your career will invariably contribute to a more engaged, productive, and successful professional life.

5.6. An Invincible Combo for Career Growth

Discovering the sweet spot between mindfulness and resilience can be the key to unlocking an entirely new level of personal and career growth. When you learn to quiet your mind and intensify your focus, you can face adversity head-on with exquisite calm and undeterred resolve. Remember, resilience is not about avoiding the storm but learning to dance in the rain. Through the consistent application of mindfulness practices, you not only become dance-proficient in all weather conditions, but you enter the storm fully equipped and prepared. And that's when you truly start thriving in the face of challenges.

Immerse into this empowering journey towards mindfulness-inspired resilience and witness the dawning of your best self, armed and ready to tackle all professional challenges that come your way. As you cultivate mindfulness and feed your resilient nature, you'll realize just how potent this duo can be in charting your path to sustained career success. Embrace the techniques, strategies, and anecdotes provided within this chapter as a roadmap for your journey. Be patient, persistent, and engaged in your practice, and before you know it, you'll be living the miraculous results of your mindful resilience every single day.

Chapter 6. Allaying Anxiety: The Role of Mindfulness in Stress Management

A constant companion in today's fast-paced world is the distressing and sometimes paralyzing force known as 'Anxiety'. This mental syndrome of sorts has the potential to restrain individuals from reaching their full potential, often clouding their judgment and keeping them stuck in a cycle of stress. However, with mindfulness as a powerful tool, we can learn to manage and even ease the overwhelming pressures exerted by anxiety, ultimately helping to create a needful shift towards positivity and productivity.

6.1. Mindfulness: A Fundamental Overview

Before diving into the heart of the matter, it's crucial to understand mindfulness in its core essence. Mindfulness is the practice that involves focussing fully on the present moment, thereby aiding you to accept it without any judgment. It's about paying attention to your thoughts, feelings, and surroundings, acknowledging them openly, and letting them pass without any reaction. This mindful awareness can help you remain balanced and calm, even during the stressful episodes.

6.2. The Anatomy of Anxiety

Anxiety is a complex emotional response, often driven by our brain's natural 'fight or flight' instinct to protect against perceived dangers. It often manifests as dread or apprehension about what's to come. When confronted with a threat, your body releases adrenaline, leading to physical signs of anxiety such as rapid heartbeat, quick breathing, and increased alertness. For some, this response is triggered excessively or unnecessarily, causing persistent anxiety which can impede daily life and career aspirations.

6.3. How Mindfulness Alleviates Anxiety

Mindfulness, with its inherent quality of fostering a non-judgmental awareness of the present moment, is uniquely positioned to combat anxiety. It pursues the idea of taking control of your thoughts rather than allowing them to control you. With regular mindfulness practices, you develop a certain kind of detachment from your fears and worries, allowing you to observe your thoughts and emotions from a bystander's perspective rather than being embroiled in them.

A pivotal aspect of employing mindfulness for reducing anxiety is that it encourages acknowledgement of anxiety-provoking thoughts without reacting to them or trying to suppress them. If we continuously attempt to push away 'negative' thoughts, we intensify our brain's perception of threat, fueling further anxiety. Instead, mindfulness helps in gently acknowledging these thoughts without feeding them with additional energy, thus breaking the cycle of stress potentiation that underlies chronic anxiety.

6.4. Mindfulness Techniques for Anxiety Management

There are several methods through which mindfulness can be practiced effectively for countering anxiety. A daily routine, even as short as 5 to 10 minutes, can be highly beneficial.

- Body Scan: This technique requires you to pay close attention to different parts of your body. Starting from the head and ending at the toes, each section of your body is closely scanned. It increases your awareness of the body, grounding you to present reality.

- Mindful Breathing: Focusing on your breath can help calm your mind. It involves taking slow, deep breaths and paying full attention to the breathing cycle.

- Mindful Walking: Practicing mindfulness while walking brings your attention to the sensations of your steps and engages your body with the current activity, steering away from anxiety-inducing thoughts.

- Guided Imagery: In this technique, you imagine a place or situation that is calming and serene. You can use a guided imagery script or audio recordings to help navigate through the process.

6.5. The Role of Mindful Meditation in Workplace Stress Management

Office environments are ripe with potential stressors, from looming deadlines to tense team dynamics. Embracing mindfulness meditation techniques can help employees cultivate stress resilience and lead to improved productivity.

Mindful meetings, for instance, where each member takes a moment of silence to focus on their breath before discussing the agenda, can encourage a more relaxed, cooperative atmosphere. Likewise, employees can be encouraged to take short mindful breaks during their workday to defuse accumulating tensions and to reconnect with their tasks refreshed.

6.6. Mindfulness as a Progressive Career Strategy

While mindfulness might initially seem to be oriented towards personal well-being, its positive effects spill over into your professional life as well. It helps enhance critical soft skills like communication, leadership, and emotional intelligence. For example, with mindful listening, you can better understand your colleagues' perspectives, fostering improved teamwork and conflict resolution.

Moreover, the constant state of calm and focused awareness that mindfulness ushers in can boost creativity, decision-making skills, and overall work performance: qualities invariably essential for career advancement.

As much as embedding mindfulness practices into your lifestyle can be challenging, the rewards in terms of anxiety management and career growth are worth the effort. A mindful approach can serve as a compass, guiding you past the tumultuous waters of anxiety towards the tranquil bay of career success. So, let's begin this journey of mindful living today and undertake the first step in transforming the way we manage our anxieties and, by extension, our lives.

Chapter 7. Communication with Clarity: Mindful Interactions at Work

In the professional landscape, the value of clear communication is immeasurable. In fact, it is one of the key drivers propelling organizations towards their objectives. In this context, the ancient practice of mindfulness can play a tremendous role in enhancing clarity in communication. How? Let's delve deeper.

7.1. The Nexus of Mindfulness and Communication

Recognizing the significance of mindfulness starts with understanding its core concept. Mindfulness is the practice of intentionally focusing on the present moment, calmly acknowledging and accepting one's feelings, thoughts, and bodily sensations. As you internalize this perception, it has profound implications when applied to communication.

In a corporate setting, being mindful translates into being fully aware of the present interactions, understanding the recipient's perspective, and responding consciously. This practice of enhanced 'here and now' attention results in thoughtful, effective communication, fostering an environment primed for constructive dialogue and interpersonal understanding.

7.2. Approaches to Mindful Communication

The integration of mindfulness in communication can be

implemented following a few key approaches:

1. Active Listening: This involves a higher degree of listening that involves full attention to the speaker and the context of the discussion.

2. Non-verbal Recognition: Mindful communication isn't just about words—it's about being aware of non-verbal cues, such as tone of voice, facial expressions, and body language.

3. Reflective Responses: Before responding, taking a pause to reflect allows you to articulate your ideas more clearly, reinforcing the effectiveness of the exchange.

7.3. The Impact of Mindful Communication in the Workplace

Mindfulness can have a transformative impact on workplace communication, some of the key benefits include:

1. Enhanced Understanding: Mindful communication leads to the accurate decoding of messages, reducing the chances of misinterpretations or misinformation.

2. Improved Relationships: By fostering mutual respect and shared understanding, mindful communication strengthens relationships, creating a harmonious work environment that fosters collaboration.

3. Reduced Conflicts: Mindful communication allows for conscious responses, reducing knee-jerk reactions that can lead to unnecessary conflicts.

Each of these impacts contributes to a culture of transparency, understanding, and mutual respect, which are foundational to organizational success.

7.4. Developing Mindful Communication Habits

Developing a habit of mindful communication can begin with these practical steps:

1. Practice Active Listening: Start by fully attuning to the speaker. Try to clear your mind of any possible distractions and focus completely on the conversation at hand.

2. Be Empathic: Try to perceive the situation from the speaker's viewpoint. Empathy is a valuable tool in mindful communication; it helps in understanding the speaker's intent and emotional state.

3. Self Awareness: Be aware of your own reactions and emotions. Self-awareness is key to managing your responses effectively.

Integrating these steps within your routine interactions can aid in establishing a pattern of mindful communication.

7.5. Conclusion

Mindfulness is a journey, not a destination. Therefore, developing mindfulness-based communication might not happen overnight. It calls for intentional practice and consistent effort. But the benefits of clearer, more effective communication are worth the effort.

Empower your career with communication rooted in mindfulness! This can not only aid personal development but also have a ripple effect, enhancing the overall productivity and wellbeing of your organization. As you progress on this journey, remember that the road to success isn't always easy—that's why it leads to places not everyone can reach.

Chapter 8. Mindfulness as a Leadership Tool: Guiding Teams with Empathy

We live in an era of constant distractions, relentless multitasking, overloaded inboxes, and unpredictable challenges that can tax even the most resilient leader's capacities. In this volatile mix, the danger of leadership burnout is genuine, and the cost of this to organizations is significant.

Mindfulness, the practice of intentional, non-judgmental focus on the current moment, can be an invaluable tool in our leadership toolkit. Surprising to some, mindfulness is not about taking mini-vacations from our pressing work; instead, it's a way of effectively engaging with that work using the entire range of our human capacities.

8.1. The Intersection of Leadership and Mindfulness

Leaders play a pivotal role within an organization. Their guidance, actions, decisions, and, often, their mere presence can significantly impact the work environment and team performance. In such a critical role, leaders often shoulder immense pressure accompanied by incessant demands on their time and mental resources.

This constant pull of attention can lead to a kind of "tunnel vision," where perspective narrows and critical thinking and decision-making skills can suffer. Herein, mindfulness can serve as a gateway to a more balanced, resilient approach to leadership. By staying present and aware, leaders can maintain a broader viewpoint, stay open to new ideas, and make decisions that are both strategic and empathetic.

8.2. The Ethos of Mindful Leadership

Mindful leadership is not about transforming you into an entirely different kind of leader or person. Instead, it's about becoming more of who you already are and realizing more of your current capacities – including your capacity for awareness, clarity, focus, creativity, compassion, and courage.

Leaders practicing mindfulness remain present and attain a degree of tranquility amidst chaos. This stillness does not imply lethargy or apathy, but rather a calm, centered focus that enables the leader to navigate turbulent waters effectively. They avoid impulsive decisions, instead favoring thought-out strategies and responses.

Furthermore, they exhibit higher empathy towards their teams, understanding and acknowledging individual feelings and team morale, which resonates in enhanced team dynamics and performance.

8.3. Implementing Mindful Leadership Practices

Revolutionizing leadership with mindfulness is not an overnight transformation. It requires practice, persistence, and patience. Here are some strategies to help you get started on your path to mindful leadership:

8.4. Embracing Empathy in Leadership

Practice mindful decision-making: Rather than rushing to judgement, consider gathering diverse perspectives and options. This plays out in better team decisions, as you learn to navigate the balance of assertiveness and open-mindedness necessary for effective decision-making.

Empathy is not just beneficial, but essential for effective leadership. Empathic leaders understand their team's needs, concerns, and perspectives, fostering a supportive and collaborative work environment that cultivates trust and respect. By practicing mindfulness, a leader naturally tends to become more empathetic, and vice versa – a positive feedback loop is established.

A mindful leader doesn't simply dictate; rather, they facilitate, motivate, and interact on a deeper level with their team. They embody and promote a culture of respect and understanding.

8.5. Navigating Challenges Mindfully

Difficulties and challenges are par for the course in any leadership role. Mindful leaders face these tests with resilience and poise. They appreciate that setbacks are opportunities for growth and learning and approach them not with trepidation but with curiosity and the readiness to glean insights. This does not mean they enjoy or invite adversity—but they meet it head-on when it arrives.

In conclusion, practicing mindfulness in leadership fosters a harmonious work culture, bolsters decision-making skills, and enhances productivity and creativity. As leaders become more mindful, they unlock their potential and that of their teams, paving the way for continuous growth, improvement, and success. Mindful leadership isn't a switch to be flicked on—it's a journey to embark on, a lifestyle choice made every day with practice and perseverance.

Chapter 9. Work-life Wellness: Striking Balance Through Mindfulness

Workplace wellness is much more than simply achieving professional objectives. It extends to the quality of your work, your interaction with colleagues, and your overall satisfaction in your role. In this modern, fast-paced era, striking the perfect balance between work and personal life can be a significant challenge. Incorporating mindfulness into your daily routine can usher in a profound sense of peace, improve focus, and ultimately help you strike a balance in your work-life wellness.

9.1. The Impetus for Mindfulness

First, let's understand why mindfulness should be the norm rather than the exception. As our workplaces become increasingly demanding, individuals often find themselves splitting their attention between multiple tasks. This scatterbrained approach can lead to reduced productivity and increased stress levels.

Mindfulness encourages us to slow down, focus on one task at a time, and fully engage with it. This approach reduces the chances of burnout and puts us in a better position to manage stress and ultimately, improve work-life balance.

9.2. Navigating Stress through Mindfulness

High levels of stress can impair our overall well-being, specifically mental health. Mindfulness can be used as a tool to mitigate stress by focusing on the present moment, avoiding negative thought spirals that can augment stress.

Creating a personal mindfulness routine could involve allocating specific times each day for mindfulness activities. It could be as simple as practicing deep-breathing for 5 minutes every hour or taking a short break to step outside and appreciate nature. Routine grounding exercises can also elevate your sense of mental well-being, breathing life into an otherwise stressful work routine.

9.3. Elevating Productivity with Mindfulness

Mindfulness can have a profound impact on productivity levels. By focusing on the task at hand and minimizing distractions, mindfulness can increase your overall output quality. Regular mindfulness breaks can also prevent mental fog, rejuvenating the mind and facilitating clearer, more innovative thinking.

9.4. Establishing Mindful Communication

In the workplace, healthy relationships and clear communication are crucial. Mindfulness encourages thoughtful, intentional communication, thereby fostering an environment of collaboration and mutual respect.

By practicing active listening and offering thoughtful responses, we not only improve workplace relationships but also potentiate effective problem-solving and innovation.

9.5. Balancing Work-Life Wellness

Achieving work-life balance is a personal journey. Mindfulness practices can help individuals identify their needs and values, forming a path to a more balanced life.

This might involve implementing mini-breaks throughout the day, practicing intentional technology breaks, and setting clear boundaries between "work" and "home" environments. By anchoring yourself in present experiences rather than worrying about the past or future, you can achieve higher levels of satisfaction in both your personal and professional life.

9.6. Cultivating Resilience through Mindfulness

Resilience, often known as the ability to bounce back from adversity, is key to maintaining work-life wellness. Mindfulness equips individuals with the tools to handle stress and setbacks effectively.

Through mindfulness, individuals can develop a more flexible mindset – one that allows them to learn from challenges instead of getting overwhelmed. This shift in perspective can equip you with the ability to adapt to changes and uncertainties, a vital skill in today's ever-evolving work environment.

9.7. Incorporating Mindfulness into Daily Routine

Incorporating mindfulness doesn't have to be a colossal endeavor. It simply involves making small, consistent changes. This could include starting your day with mindfulness meditation or implementing mindful eating habits. Over time, you'll find that these habits integrate into your routine, contributing greatly to overall work-life wellness.

To conclude, mindfulness serves as an effective tool to strike a balance in your work-life wellness. Remember, even small steps towards mindfulness can leave an indelible impact on your productivity, stress levels, and overall ability to manage the delicate intricacies of your professional and personal life.

Remember to be patient with yourself during this journey as mastering mindfulness takes time. As you continue to nurture these changes, you are bound to see the blossoming of a more sustainable, satisfying work-life equilibrium. When harnessed effectively, the power of conscious living can truly propel us into new realms of wellbeing and success.

Chapter 10. The Science Behind Mindfulness: Evidence-Based Benefits and Applications

Over the past few years, mindfulness has become not just a popular term but a crucial buzzword in the professional as well as personal circles. Its popularity does not stem from being a trendy, modern term but from its proven benefits backed by a significant body of scientific research. Mindfulness is more than just being present; it involves observing the present without judgement, connecting deeply with what is happening right now, and accepting it whether we perceive it as good or bad.

10.1. The Neurology of Mindfulness

Understandably, our first dive into the science behind mindfulness begins in the brain. The brain's neuroplastic nature, its ability to rewire and adapt based on our thoughts and actions, plays a significant role in mindfulness practice.

Neuroscience has illuminated the significant alterations mindfulness can bring to brain structure and function. For example, regular mindfulness practices over an eight-week period have been found to increase cortical thickness in the hippocampus, which is responsible for learning and memory, and in specific areas related to self-referential thought and emotion regulation. Simultaneously, it has been reported to decrease brain cell volume in the amygdala, the region responsible for fear, anxiety, and stress. These changes collectively lead to improved focus, creativity, resilience, and emotional intelligence, essential skills in the workplace.

Moreover, studies using functional magnetic resonance imaging (fMRI) have shown that mindfulness can change the way different regions in the brain communicate with each other. This means that the brain can function differently, often more efficiently, even when someone is not actively practicing mindfulness.

10.2. Applications in Stress Reduction

Stress is ubiquitous in the modern workplace, with deadline pressures, workload issues, and constant organisational changes. Incorporating mindfulness practices effectively counteracts these stressors and improves mental wellbeing.

One of the most robust lines of evidence for the benefits of mindfulness is its impact on stress reduction. Mindfulness-Based Stress Reduction (MBSR), a structured program that combines mindfulness meditation and yoga, has been widely validated for its effectiveness. A meta-analysis of 20 studies found that MBSR leads to decreases in psychological stress, anxiety, and depression.

Mindfulness also diminishes the release of the stress hormone cortisol. Reduced cortisol levels are beneficial for overall health, as chronic heightened levels can lead to various health issues including sleep problems, weight gain, and cognitive difficulties.

10.3. Influence on Emotional Intelligence

Mindfulness has a remarkable influence on our ability to understand, use, and manage our emotions.

Numerous studies have touted the considerable influence mindfulness practice has on emotional intelligence (EI). EI, a key factor in developing leadership skills, encompasses self-awareness, self-regulation, motivation, empathy, and social skills. Mindfulness enhances all these factors by making us more attuned to our own feelings and those of others. For example, practicing mindfulness can improve empathy by fostering our ability to listen without judgment, a vital skill when dealing with colleagues.

10.4. Enhancing Creativity

Mindfulness doesn't just help us combat stress and become emotionally intelligent; it can also enhance creativity, which is an increasingly valuable asset in the innovative workplace of the 21st century.

Numerous studies have highlighted that mindfulness boosts various dimensions of creativity. For instance, being present-oriented and accepting, two key components of mindfulness, help to reduce cognitive rigidity — an inability to think outside the conventional paths or boxes. This fosters divergent thinking, allowing new and innovative ideas to flow.

10.5. From Theory to Practice

Finally, armed with the science, let's not forget about the practical aspects of mindfulness. There are numerous ways to practice it, with something to suit everyone. Some people might find sitting quietly and focusing on their breath beneficial, while others might prefer walking meditation, mindful eating, or yoga. What's most important is that the individual finds a method that they can commit to practicing regularly.

In conclusion, mindfulness offers a world of benefits backed by solid scientific evidence. Whether you're looking to relieve stress, improve emotional intelligence, or boost creativity, the practice can be an incredibly valuable tool. The practice of mindfulness and fostering a mindful approach to working and professional relationships can transform the dynamics of your career in ways you can only imagine and cultivate your pathway to sustained success.

Chapter 11. Sustaining Success: Mindful Practices for a Lifetime of Achievement

Achievement in one's career path often involves transcending traditional methods of growth and development. A crucial aspect of this transcendence is employing mindfulness. The following sections delve deeper into how mindful practices can help you sustain success throughout your life.

11.1. Understanding Mindfulness

Mindfulness refers to the practice of directing our attention to our inner and outer experiences at the present moment. It embodies being fully awake in life, perceiving the richness of each moment of existence. Mindfulness is about focusing our attention, which we can accomplish through purposeful strategies, exercises, and habits. An essential element of mindfulness includes observing our own thoughts and feelings without judgment. Rather than being swept away in thought or emotion, mindfulness helps us detach and observe, fostering an increased sense of clarity and control.

11.2. The Power of Mindful Attention

Mindful attention is a powerful tool that can significantly impact your personal and professional life. By managing our attention intentionally, we can shift from being reactive to being responsive. This shift allows our minds to become more tranquil, enhancing our capacity to make thoughtful decisions and solve problems more effectively. Moreover, being mindful helps in reducing stress and managing difficult emotions, both key factors in enhancing productivity and maintaining psychological wellbeing in the workplace.

11.3. Integrating Mindfulness Into Your Daily Life

Bringing mindfulness into your life involves more than just setting aside a few minutes each day for meditation. It is about practicing presence in every moment. Initially, you can create space for mindfulness by focusing on your breath, a physical sensation, or even a daily activity such as washing dishes or taking a walk. Consider the experience using all your senses.

11.4. Mindful Communication

Mindful communication is another fundamental aspect of integrating mindfulness into your professional life. It means actively and fully listening when someone is speaking, not interrupting them, and responding in a thoughtful and clear manner. This approach to communication can foster better understanding and relationships in the workplace, contributing to a healthier, more effective work environment.

11.5. Mindful Leadership

Mindful leadership is an approach that equips leaders with the tools and techniques to be more effective in managing themselves and leading others. A mindful leader cultivates focus, clarity, creativity, and empathy. These leaders aren't just focused on short-term gains but also on the long-term wellbeing and success of their teams. By being present, they foster a culture of respect, openness, and innovation.

11.6. Mindfulness and Creativity

Improvements to creativity, one of the most desirable yet elusive traits, can also be achieved through mindfulness. The practice fosters an open, curious state of mind, where new ideas can be freely explored and nurtured. Embracing mindfulness means accepting all thoughts and ideas without judgment, creating an environment that facilitates creativity and fosters innovation.

11.7. Sustaining Success through Mindfulness

Incorporating mindfulness into our daily lives and work can lead to monumental changes in our overall wellbeing and success. By practicing mindfulness, we allow ourselves to refine our attention, cultivate a better emotional state and foster a more innovative and productive mindset.

Yet, like any other skill, mindfulness needs continuous practice for it to become an integral part of our lives and for us to reap its benefits. After all, the path to sustained success isn't a destination, but rather an ongoing journey of growth and improvement. Constantly refining your mindset and traits through mindfulness ensures that you keep advancing professionally while also growing personally.

In conclusion, incorporating mindfulness into your daily habits may not only enhance your career performance but also significantly improve personal growth and mental clarity. The power to sustain success lies within our minds and how effectively we can harness our potential to develop and maintain a mindful approach to life and work. Embrace mindfulness and unlock unparalleled growth in your journey to success.

www.ingramcontent.com/pod-product-compliance
Lightning Source LLC
Chambersburg PA
CBHW072219290526
45794CB00007B/2813